Valentine Pugs

50 Coloring Designs of Adorable and Lovable Pugs

Curly Pug Tails® Press

This book belongs to:

This book has been designed for coloring. Be as creative and colorful as you like — technicolor is good! Each coloring page has a framed blank page on its flip side to use as you wish — doodling, journaling, sketching, holiday thoughts — or anything else you can think of.

Enjoy!

HUG
ME
HUG
ME
HUG
ME
HUG
ME

I LOVE YOU
YOU'LL DO

IT'S NOT
Dog Hair
IT'S
Pug
GLITTER

HAPPY
VALENTINES DAY

I LOVE MY
PUG

XOXO

LOVE
BUG

LOVE

I LOVE YOU

PUGS
&
KISSES

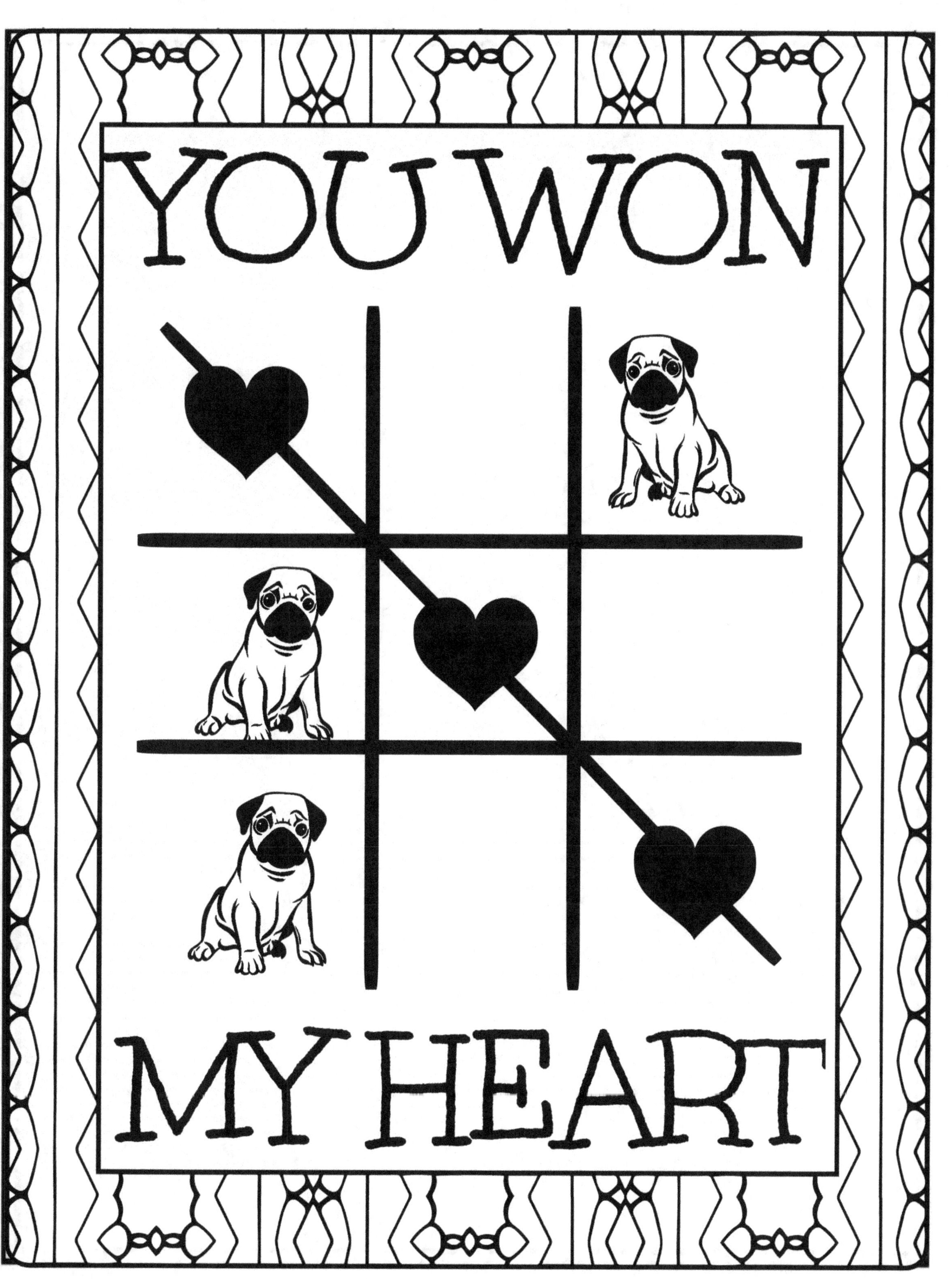
YOU WON
MY HEART

I WOOF YOU TO THE MOON AND BACK
I LOVE YOU

Valentine's
Day

I LOVE YOU

HUG
ME

SMILE

You are my
happiness!

I PUGGIN'
LOVE
YOU

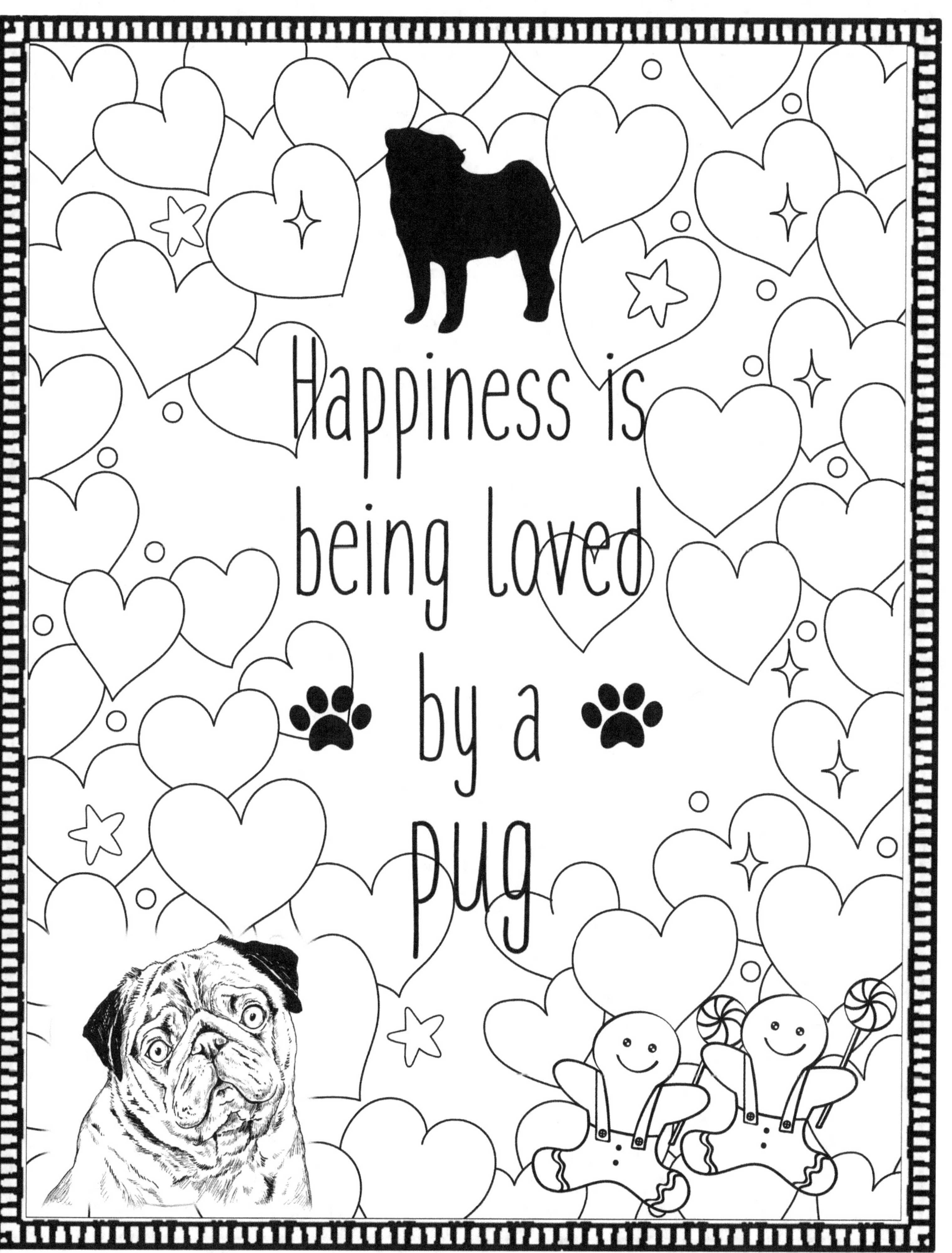

Happiness is
being loved
by a
pug

LOVE
BUG

Always
KISS
YOUR
PUG
GOODNIGHT

HUGS

A HUNK
A HUNK OF PUGGIN' LOVE

I STEAL HEARTS

XOXO

LOVE BUG
I LOVE YOU
BE MINE
SWEET PEA
HUG ME
XOXO
BEAR HUG
SMILE

YOU MAKE MY
HEART SING